# Mistake-Proofing for Operators

## The ZQC System

SHOPFLOOR SERIES

# Mistake-Proofing for Operators

## The ZQC System

Created by
The Productivity Press
Development Team

Based on
*Zero Quality Control:
Source Inspection and
the Poka-Yoke System*
by Shigeo Shingo

**Productivity Press**
Portland, Oregon

Adapted from Shigeo Shingo, *Zero Quality Control: Source Inspection and the Poka-Yoke System*, English edition © 1986 by Productivity Press (based on *Furyo = zero e no chosen: genryu kensa to poka-yoke shisutemu; zero QC hoshiki e no tenkai*, © 1985 by the Japan Management Association; originally translated by Andrew P. Dillon).

Additional copies of this book are available from the publisher. Discounts are available for multiple copies through the Sales Department (800-394-6868). Address all other inquiries to:

Productivity Press
P.O. Box 13390
Portland OR 97213-0390
United States of America
Telephone: 503-235-0600
Telefax: 503-235-0909
E-mail: service@ppress.com

Instructional design and editing by Elizabeth S. MacDonell, Write One Consulting
Book and cover design by William Stanton
Cover illustration by Gary Ragaglia
Cover preparation by Gretchen Long
Cartoons by Matthew C. DeMaio
Illustrations and graphics by Gordon Ekdahl, FineLine Illustration and Graphic Design
Additional design and composition by William H. Brunson, Typography Services
Printed and bound by BookCrafters in the United States of America

*Library of Congress Cataloging-in-Publication Data*

Mistake-proofing for operators : the ZQC system / created by the Productivity Press
    development team.
            p.     cm. — (Shopfloor series)
        "Based on Zero quality control ... by Shigeo Shingō."
        Includes bibliographical references.
        ISBN 1-56327-127-3 (paperback)
        1. Quality control.   2. Process control.   I. Shingō, Shigeo,
1909–1990.   Furyō zero e no chōsen. English.   II. Productivity Press.
III. Series.
TS156.M535   1996
658.5′62—dc20                                                    96-27569
                                                                    CIP

01  00  99  98  97     10  9  8  7  6  5  4  3  2

# Contents

# Chapter 3. Basic Elements of the ZQC System

# Chapter 4. Using Poka-Yoke Systems

# Chapter 5. Examples of Poka-Yoke Applications

# Chapter 6. Reflections and Conclusions

# Preface

The book you are holding is intended to give you powerful knowledge that you can use to make your workplace more productive, and your job simpler and more satisfying. It's about a way to manufacture or assemble products that have *zero defects* by catching and fixing human mistakes and machine errors before they can cause defects. The mistake-proofing approach you will learn about here is called Zero Quality Control (ZQC for short). Zero Quality Control does not mean *no* quality control. On the contrary, it means quality control that ensures zero defects, period—not just a reduction in defects.

ZQC has been used by leading Japanese companies for many years. It is one of the secrets of low-inventory production, since no defects means no need for buffer inventory to replace defective products. Today many leading Western manufacturers also use mistake-proofing techniques. The ZQC system you will learn about here is the most effective approach for mistake-proofing. It can eliminate wastes related to quality defects—rework, scrap, and equipment downtime—and maintain the company's good reputation with its customers. ZQC supports the company's competitiveness and makes production and assembly work easier.

One of the great things about ZQC is that it focuses on correcting the conditions for processing, not on blaming people for making mistakes. Shigeo Shingo, the developer of ZQC, recognized that it is human nature to make mistakes or forget things. People should not be punished for mistakes. Punishment only makes people feel bad—it doesn't eliminate defects.

The solution Dr. Shingo came up with is explained in *Mistake-Proofing for Operators*. Chapter 1 is like an "owner's manual" that tells you how to get the most out of your reading by using margin assists, summaries, and other features to help you pull out what you need to know. Chapter 2 describes the benefits of zero defects for companies and employees. It tells about five different causes of defects, and introduces the idea of a check before processing to catch unpredictable mistakes that could turn into defects.

Chapter 3 goes into more detail about this unusual idea of doing inspection *before* the process instead of afterward. This kind of inspection before processing is called *source inspection,* and this chapter compares it with other kinds of inspection like Statistical Quality Control. This chapter goes on to introduce the other three "basics" of ZQC: 100 percent inspection, quick feedback and action, and poka-yoke systems. *100 percent inspection* refers to the approach of checking every single unit of product, not just a sampling. *Quick feedback and action* means a system for immediately informing someone that there is a problem so they can do something about it before a defect is made.

In ZQC, the first three basics are carried out with *poka-yoke systems.* These systems use simple, often inexpensive sensing devices to make sure the inspection happens every time. They also give immediate feedback, such as stopping the equipment or giving a warning. Limit switches and guide pins are two kinds of poka-yoke devices you will read about in Chapter 4. Chapter 5 presents before and after examples of poka-yoke applications. Test out your own ideas about mistake-proofing solutions by covering the bottom part of each page while you think about the situation described at the top.

Chapter 6 wraps up with final reflections questions and resources to help you learn more about mistake-proofing and ZQC.

Dr. Shingo often taught ZQC by telling stories about how people approach quality control. Everyone can relate to the managers and employees he told about. Like most of us, they were used to seeing things in a certain way. In Shingo's stories, you could just picture the cartoon light bulb turning on when people realized there was a better way to do the job. We hope this book captures some of the flavor of his thinking.

*Mistake-Proofing for Operators* was developed from Dr. Shingo's book, *Zero Quality Control: Source Inspection and the Poka-Yoke System,* which was written for managers. When you get right down to it, though, you—the frontline production and assembly associates—are the people who know best what problems arise during production and have good ideas what to do about them. Many of the mistake-proofing examples you will read about were developed by shopfloor employees like you. In many cases operators and assembly associates participate in installing mistake-proofing devices on existing equipment—or work with engineers and designers to plan mistake-proofing systems into new equipment or processes. Since you have the most to gain from applying ZQC, we have developed this book specifically to give you the basics in a straightforward and interesting format. Once you understand these basics, you can see how they might apply to your specific situation at work.

One of the most effective ways to use this book is to read and discuss it with other employees in group learning sessions. We have deliberately planned the book so that it can be used this way, with chunks of information that can be covered in a series of short sessions or in one longer event. (Most chapters can be covered in a single session.) Each chapter includes reflection questions to stimulate group discussion. A Learning Package is also available, which includes a leader's guide, a copy of Dr. Shingo's book *Zero Quality Control*, overhead transparencies to summarize major points, and color slides showing examples of ZQC applications in different companies.

The Zero Quality Control approach is simple and universal. It works in companies all over the world. Today, the basic principles of ZQC have been used to eliminate defects in all types of manufacturing, assembly, and even service industries. We hope this book and Learning Package will tell you what you need to know to be involved in a mistake-proofing implementation and show you how ZQC can make your workplace a better place to spend your time.

## Acknowledgments

We at Productivity deeply appreciate the life work of the late Shigeo Shingo, developer of the ZQC system and author of *Zero Quality Control: Source Inspection and the Poka-Yoke System*, the book on which *Mistake-Proofing for Operators* is based. Dr. Shingo's years of observation and thinking about quality control have changed the face of manufacturing around the world. We are grateful for the opportunity to share this powerful technique with a wider audience.

This book is modeled after the instructional design developed for *5S for Operators* (Productivity Press, 1996) by Melanie Rubin of Productivity, Inc. Many people contributed to the design, editing, and content of that pioneering Shopfloor Series book. In particular, Dee Tadlock of Read Right Systems gave extensive instructional design input and review to this series. The form and content of the Shopfloor Series books have been heavily influenced by input from Productivity customers, including participants in focus groups, readers who reviewed the manuscript, and respondents to our telephone survey. Special thanks to Bruce Hamilton of United Electric Controls Company for his input on source inspection.

The development of *Mistake-Proofing for Operators* has been a strong team effort. Within Productivity Press, Steven Ott and Diane Asay played major roles in the product definition, development, and editorial stages. Karen Jones served as project manager, with text extraction and development by instructional designer Liz MacDonell of Write One Consulting. Bill Stanton created the book and cover design, with cover composition by Gretchen Long and cover illustration by Gary Ragaglia of The Vision Group. Susan Swanson managed the prepress production and manufacturing, with editorial assistance from Pauline Sullivan. Page composition and additional design was done by William H. Brunson, Typography Services. Graphic illustrations were created by Gordon Ekdahl, FineLine Illustration and Graphic Design, and cartoon illustrations were designed and created by Matthew C. DeMaio.

Finally, the staff at Productivity Press wishes to acknowledge the good work of the many people who are now in the process of implementing the ZQC system in their own organizations. We welcome any feedback about this book, as well as input about how we can continue to serve you in your ZQC implementation efforts.

# Chapter 1

## Getting Started

### CHAPTER OVERVIEW

**Purpose of This Book**

**What This Book Is Based On**

**Two Ways to Use This Book**

**How to Get the Most Out of Your Reading**

- Becoming Familiar with This Book as a Whole
- Becoming Familiar with Each Chapter
- Using a Reading Strategy
- Using the Margin Assists

**Overview of the Contents**

**In Conclusion**

- Summary
- Reflections

## Purpose of This Book

Key Point

*Mistake-Proofing for Operators: The ZQC System* was written to give you the information you need to participate in implementing the ZQC system in your workplace. ZQC is short for *Zero Quality Control*. The goal of ZQC is to make products with zero defects.

## What This Book Is Based On

BACKGROUND

*Mistake-Proofing for Operators* is based on Shigeo Shingo's book called *Zero Quality Control: Source Inspection and the Poka-Yoke System*, also published by Productivity Press (see Figure 1-1).

It took Dr. Shingo 26 years to develop the ZQC system. As he studied the production operations of many factories, he discovered two important facts that are the basis of ZQC:

1. No matter how good you are at finding defects, no matter how thoroughly you follow up with corrective action, improving your defect inspection and feedback process will not prevent defects from happening in the first place.

2. To prevent defects you must look at the process to determine what condition leads to the defect, then control that condition.

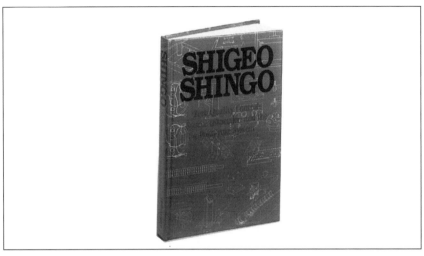

Figure 1-1. *Zero Quality Control: Source Inspection and the Poka-Yoke System*

The book you are currently reading presents the main concepts and tools of Dr. Shingo's book in a shortened and simplified version that requires less time and effort to read than the original book.

The original book is useful as a reference for more detailed information, including case studies on implementing ZQC in various kinds of workplaces.

## Two Ways to Use This Book

There are at least two ways to use this book:

1. As the reading material for a learning group or study group process within your company.

2. For learning on your own.

Productivity Press offers a Learning Package that uses *Mistake-Proofing for Operators* as the foundation reading material for a learning group. Your company may decide instead to design its own learning group process based on *Mistake-Proofing for Operators*. Or, you may read this book for individual learning without formal group discussion.

# How to Get the Most Out of Your Reading

## Becoming Familiar with This Book as a Whole

There are a few steps you can follow to make it easier to absorb the information in this book. We've included a suggested amount of time for each step, but take as much time as you need to become familiar with the material.

*How-to Steps*

1. Scan the Table of Contents to see how *Mistake-Proofing for Operators* is set up. (1 minute)

2. Read the rest of this chapter for an overview of the book's contents. (5 minutes)

3. Flip through the book to get a feel for its style, flow, and design. Notice how the chapters are structured and glance at the pictures. (5 minutes)

4. Read parts of Chapter 6, "Reflections and Conclusions," to get a sense for the book's direction. (2 minutes)

## Becoming Familiar with Each Chapter

For each chapter in *Mistake-Proofing for Operators* we suggest you follow these steps to get the most out of your reading:

*How-to Steps*

1. Read the "Chapter Overview" on the first page to get a feel for the path the chapter follows. (1 minute)

2. Flip through the chapter, looking at the way it is laid out. (1 minute)

3. Ask yourself, Based on what I've seen in this chapter so far, what questions do I have about the material? (3 minutes)

4. Now read the chapter. How long this takes depends on what you already know about the content, and what you are trying to get out of your reading. Enhance your reading by doing the following:

   • Use the margin assists to help you follow the flow of information (see the description on page 7).

   • If the book is your own, use a highlighter to mark key information and answers to your questions about the material. If the book is not your own, take notes on a separate piece of paper.

   • Answer the Take Five questions in the text. These will help you absorb the information by reflecting on how you can implement it.

5. Read the "Chapter Summary" to confirm what you have learned. If you don't remember something in the summary, find that section in the chapter and review it. (5 minutes)

6. Finally, read the "Reflections" questions at the end of the chapter. Think about these questions and write down your answers. (5 minutes)

---

## TAKE FIVE

Take a few minutes to think about these questions and to write down your answers:

- What is the overall purpose of this book?

- How might you become familiar with the structure of the book and of each chapter?

Figure 1-2. Giving Your Brain a Framework for Learning

## Using a Reading Strategy

Key Point

Reading strategy is based on two simple points about the way people learn. The first point is this: *It's difficult for your brain to absorb new information if it does not have a structure to place it in.* As an analogy, imagine trying to build a house without putting a framework in place first.

Like building a frame for a house, you can give your brain a framework for the new information in the book by getting an overview of the contents and then flipping through the materials. Within each chapter, you repeat this process on a smaller scale by reading the overview, main points, and headings before reading the text (see Figure 1-2).

Key Point

The second point about learning is this: *It is a lot easier to learn if you take in the information one layer at a time, instead of trying to absorb it all at once.* It's like finishing the walls of a house: First you lay down a coat of primer. When it's dry, you apply a coat of paint, and later a final finish coat.

When reading a book, many people think they should start with the first word and read straight through until the end. This is not usually the best way to learn from a book. The method we've described here is easier, more fun, and more effective.

## Using the Margin Assists

As you've noticed by now, this book uses small images called *margin assists* to help you follow the information in each chapter. There are five types of margin assists:

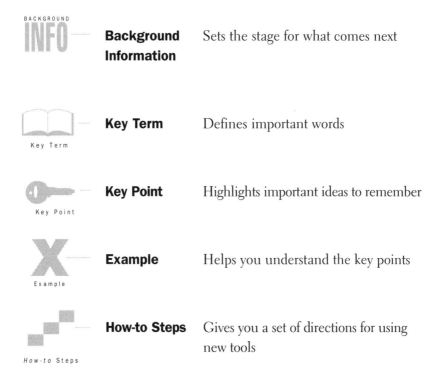

**Background Information**     Sets the stage for what comes next

**Key Term**     Defines important words

**Key Point**     Highlights important ideas to remember

**Example**     Helps you understand the key points

**How-to Steps**     Gives you a set of directions for using new tools

---

### TAKE FIVE

Take five minutes to think about these questions and to write down your answers:

- How can you help yourself learn more from this book (and other reading material in the future)?
- What are margin assists? How do you expect they will help you follow the information in the book?

# Overview of the Contents

## Chapter 1. Getting Started (pages 1-12)

This is the chapter you're reading now. It explains the purpose of *Mistake-Proofing for Operators* and how it was written. Then it gives tips for getting the most out of your reading. Finally, it gives you an overview of each chapter.

## Chapter 2. Introduction to Zero Quality Control (pages 13-22)

Chapter 2 introduces and defines *Zero Quality Control (ZQC)*. It also explains why ZQC is important for companies and how ZQC will make your work easier and more enjoyable. Finally, it explains what causes defects in the first place and how conditions can be controlled to prevent them.

## Chapter 3. Basic Elements of the ZQC System (pages 23-36)

Chapter 3 explains the four basic elements of ZQC: source inspection, 100 percent inspection, quick feedback and action on problems, and poka-yoke devices. It also gives you an overview of two traditional types of inspection and introduces you in greater detail to source inspection, an approach that catches problems before they become defects.

## Chapter 4. Using Poka-Yoke Systems (pages 37-54)

Chapter 4 describes poka-yoke systems in detail: how they are used in source inspections and informative inspections, how they regulate the process, methods for using poka-yoke systems, and types of sensing devices that are used in poka-yoke systems.

## Chapter 5. Examples of Poka-Yoke Applications (pages 55-74)

Chapter 5 presents a number of examples of poka-yoke systems in use. Exposure to a variety of applications will help you understand how poka-yoke systems are put to use and will give you ideas for how to apply them in your own workplace.

## Chapter 6. Reflections and Conclusions (pages 75-79)

Chapter 6 presents reflections on and conclusions to this book. It discusses possibilities for applying what you've learned, and suggests ways for you to create a personal action plan for implementing ZQC. Finally, it describes opportunities for further learning about ZQC.

# In Conclusion

## SUMMARY

*Mistake-Proofing for Operators: The ZQC System* is based on Shigeo Shingo's book, *Zero Quality Control: Source Inspection and the Poka-Yoke System.* You can read *Mistake-Proofing for Operators* on your own or as part of a learning group process within your company.

To get the most out of reading this book, it is important to begin by familiarizing yourself with its contents, structure, and design. Then you can follow specific steps for reading each chapter, which will make your reading more efficient, effective, and enjoyable.

This strategy is based on two principles about the way your brain learns:

1. It is difficult for your brain to absorb new information if it does not have a structure to place it in.

2. It is a lot easier to learn if you take in the information one layer at a time instead of trying to absorb it all at once.

Chapter 1, "Getting Started," is the chapter you have just read. Chapter 2 introduces ZQC, its benefits to your company and you, and several ideas about product defects that will help you understand ZQC. Chapter 3 explains the basic elements of ZQC and describes how traditional types of inspection differ from ZQC inspections. Chapter 4 explains poka-yoke systems in detail. Chapter 5 offers examples of poka-yoke systems in action. Chapter 6 presents the conclusions to this book and suggests ways for you to learn more about the ZQC system.

## REFLECTIONS

Now that you have completed this chapter, take five minutes to think about these questions and to write down your answers:

- What did you learn from reading this chapter that stands out as particularly useful or interesting?

- Do you have any questions about the topics presented in this chapter? If so, what are they?

- What information do you still need to fully understand the ideas presented in this chapter?

- How can you get this information?

# Chapter 2

## Introduction to Zero Quality Control

## What Is Zero Quality Control (ZQC)?

**Key Term**

*Zero Quality Control (ZQC)* is a quality control (QC) approach for achieving zero defects. "Zero" refers to the goal of this approach: to make products with zero defects.

**Key Point**

*ZQC is based on the principle that defects are prevented by controlling the performance of a process so that it cannot produce defects—even when a mistake is made by a machine or a person.*

ZQC is an approach that doesn't point fingers at people. It recognizes that machines and people make mistakes sometimes, and it finds ways to keep those errors from turning into defects. As the title of this book suggests, ZQC is a method for *mistake-proofing* a process.

In the following chapters you will learn what ZQC is all about and how it works. You will also learn why it is important and how it can help your workplace be more efficient—and therefore more enjoyable.

Figure 2-1: Even One Defect Can Hurt the Company's Reputation

## Why Focus on Zero Defects?

Key Point

*One important reason for producing zero-defect products is to maintain customer satisfaction and loyalty.* Even one defective product can cost a company a lot of business.

Example

For example, let's say you purchase a new TV made by Company X. If the TV you buy is defective, chances are you will exchange it for another TV made by a different manufacturer. You are also less likely to buy other products made by Company X or to recommend their products to your friends or family (see Figure 2-1). In fact, you may even speak badly of the company to others.

Key Point

Cost is another reason. *A defect always costs something,* whether it's the cost of scrapping the defect, reworking the product, or repairing equipment damage. All of these costs reduce productivity and make your company's products less competitive.

Key Point

Finally, *zero defects is a key factor in a company's ability to adopt lean production methods with smaller inventories.* Many companies build and store excess inventory as a buffer to avoid problems when defects occur. ZQC assures that defective products are not produced in the first place, which allows a company to produce exactly the number of products ordered by the customer.

Figure 2-2: ZQC Makes Work Go Smoother

## How ZQC Makes Your Work Easier

Key Point

In the ZQC system, we don't talk about "fool-proofing" the process, we talk about "mistake-proofing" it. *ZQC recognizes that it is natural for people to make mistakes,* or not to notice when an error is made or a machine acts up—it doesn't mean a person is stupid or foolish.

Key Point

This approach does not point fingers after the fact or hassle people to "do better next time." *Instead, the ZQC system uses mistake-proofing devices to keep errors from ever turning into defects.*

Producing without defects means less rework and less additional effort to make the required number of good products. Zero-defects production supports your company's reputation with customers for making a high-quality product and helps keep costs low. Good business, in turn, supports job security.

Production and assembly people have an important role in reaching the zero defects goal. Most of the mistake-proofing examples you will read about were implemented by teams that included shopfloor employees along with engineering and maintenance people. Frontline associates can also help designers plan mistake-proofing features into new products or processing equipment.

16

## What Causes Defects?

Most defects happen in one of five situations:

1. Inappropriate procedures or standards are specified when the process is planned. For example, if the wrong heat treatment temperature is specified, all products will be defective. Proper planning avoids this situation.

2. Excessive variability happens during actual operations. For example, excessive play in a machine bearing can cause occasional defects. Proper maintenance keeps this from happening.

3. Damaged or excessively variable materials might be used. The solution is to inspect the materials on receipt for defects and variability.

4. Worn machine parts (for example, bearings or tools) can lead to defects. Thorough maintenance and tool management should prevent this problem.

5. Finally, even when the first four situations are just right, simple human mistakes sometimes occur or tasks are carried out imperfectly.

**Key Point**

The first four situations can be predicted and solutions can be implemented to avoid these sources of defects. *But simple mistakes—the most frequent cause of defects—occur unpredictably.* This makes them much harder to prevent.

**Key Point**

Since the goal of ZQC is to prevent *all* defects, not just reduce the number of defects, *ZQC has developed a way to catch simple mistakes before they turn into defects.* It does this by using a control function that ensures that the necessary conditions are present to make good products. The next section tells more about the control function used in ZQC.

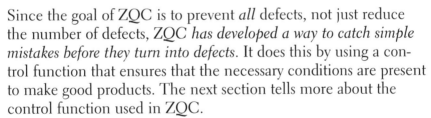

### TAKE FIVE

Take a few minutes to think about these questions and to write down your answers:

• What problems or hassles do you experience in your job as a result of defects that occur?

• What kinds of things can cause defects to happen in your process?

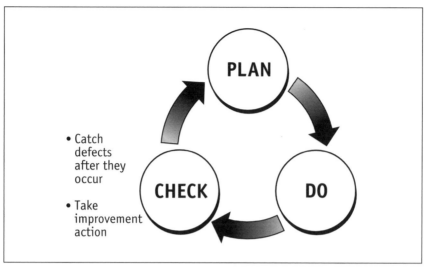

Figure 2-3: The Plan, Do, Check Cycle of the Traditional Quality Improvement Cycle

## Controlling Conditions so Defects Don't Happen

### The Traditional Quality Improvement Cycle

The "Plan, Do, Check" cycle shown in Figure 2-3 is often emphasized in traditional quality improvement activities.

In this traditional cycle, optimal processing conditions are established in the Plan stage. The planned actions then take place in the Do stage. Finally, quality monitoring is performed in the Check stage. If a defect is found, the information is fed back and corrective action is taken in the next Plan stage to improve processing conditions for the next Do cycle.

People believe that continuously repeating the functions in this cycle will lead to higher levels of quality. In fact, however, this cycle can never completely prevent defects, especially those caused by simple human or machine mistakes. *The Plan, Do, Check cycle does not provide a way to catch errors; it only gives feedback after an actual defect happens.*

Key Point

It is important to remember that an error is not the same as a defect. An error is what happens to *cause* the defect. Rather than detecting defects (which have already happened), the trick is to catch the error before it turns into a defect. ZQC solves this problem by integrating the Do and Check stages so that the plan is properly carried out.

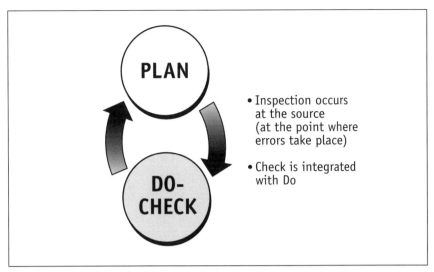

Figure 2-4: Integrating Do and Check in the Zero Quality Control Approach

## Integrating Do and Check in the ZQC Approach

ZQC recognizes that unpredictable errors can creep in between the Plan and Do functions—something happens and the plan is not carried out properly. That's why the ZQC approach integrates the Check stage with the Do stage, so that inspection takes place right at the point where problems arise. When a supervisor or worker detects an error—an operating condition that is not as it should be, for instance—he or she corrects it before the work is done. The ZQC quality cycle is shown in Figure 2-4.

ZQC combines the Check and Do stages using what we call *source inspection*—a check for proper processing conditions that is made before the processing is done. This gives instant feedback so that problems can be corrected *before* defects happen, not after.

The Zero Quality Control approach is made up of four basic elements: source inspection, 100 percent inspection, a short feedback loop, and mistake-proofing systems called *poka-yoke* (pronounced POH-kah YOH-kay). Chapter 3 describes these basic elements of ZQC in more detail.

# In Conclusion

## SUMMARY

Zero Quality Control (ZQC) is a quality control approach for achieving zero defects. ZQC is based on the principle that defects are prevented by controlling the performance of a process so that it cannot produce defects, even when a mistake is made by the machine or a human operator.

There are three main reasons for producing zero-defect products. The first reason is to maintain customer satisfaction and loyalty. The second reason is to avoid the unnecessary costs of scrap, rework, and downtime. The third reason is that zero defects is a key factor in a company's ability to adopt lean production methods with smaller inventories.

In the ZQC system, we don't talk about "fool-proofing" the process, we talk about "mistake-proofing" it. ZQC does not point fingers after the fact or hassle people to "do better next time." Instead, ZQC uses devices to keep errors from ever turning into defects in the first place.

Defects are most often caused by: (1) specification of inappropriate procedures or standards; (2) excessive variability in the operations; (3) damaged or excessively variable materials; (4) worn machine parts; or (5) simple human mistakes or tasks that are imperfectly carried out.

Simple mistakes are the most common cause of defects, and they are the hardest to prevent. Since the goal of ZQC is to prevent all defects, however, simple mistakes must be caught. This is done by way of a control function that ensures that the necessary conditions are present to make good products.

The traditional quality improvement cycle is "Plan, Do, Check." This cycle catches and corrects defects after they occur, but it can't make sure that work is done according to plan in the first place. The ZQC approach integrates the Check and Do stages. This gives instant feedback so problems can be corrected *before* defects happen.

## REFLECTIONS

Now that you have completed this chapter, take five minutes to think about these questions and to write down your answers:

- What did you learn from reading this chapter that stands out as particularly useful or interesting?

- Do you have any questions about the topics presented in this chapter? If so, what are they?

- What information do you still need to fully understand the ideas presented in this chapter?

- How can you get this information?

# Chapter 3

## Basic Elements of the ZQC System

## The Four Elements of ZQC

The ZQC system clearly recognizes that "to err is human." It's letting errors turn into defects that is the problem.

BACKGROUND

Key Point

Recall from Chapter 2 that ZQC prevents defects by integrating the Check and Do stages of the quality improvement cycle. ZQC *does this by combining four basic elements*:

1. It uses *source inspection* to catch errors before they become defects.

2. It uses *100 percent inspection* to check all of the products, not just a sample.

3. It provides *immediate feedback*, thereby shortening the time for corrective action.

4. Because smart people do make mistakes, ZQC uses *poka-yoke* (mistake-proofing) devices on processing or assembly equipment to carry out the checking function.

Key Term

The first element, *source inspection,* is the key to the ZQC control function. Source inspection assures that the conditions are in place beforehand to perform a process properly.

Source inspection is different from other types of inspection you may be familiar with, such as judgment inspection or informative inspection. To understand how source inspection works, let's first look at how these more traditional types of product inspection work.

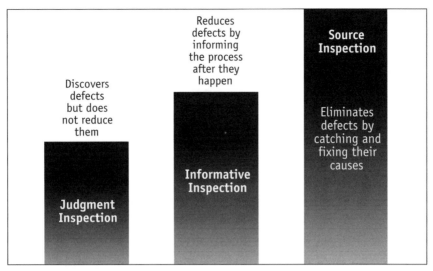

Figure 3-1: Three Approaches to Product Inspection and Their Results

## Three Approaches to Product Inspection

There are three basic approaches to the inspection of products (see Figure 3-1):

1. Inspection that discovers defects: *judgment inspection.*

2. Inspection that reduces defects: *informative inspection.*

3. Inspection that eliminates defects: *source inspection.*

Many companies use the first two kinds of inspection in their quality control programs; thus, we can consider these to be traditional types of inspection. *Only the third approach—source inspection—actually eliminates defects.*

It is important to understand the different approaches to inspection and what they do and don't do. The following sections describe traditional inspections and source inspection in more detail.

Figure 3-2: A Judgment Inspection Only Discovers Defects

## Judgment Inspections Discover Defects

**Key Term**

At many companies "quality assurance" means an inspection to catch defective products before they go out the door. The simplest approach to this is called *judgment inspection*. In a judgment inspection, a person or a machine compares the product with a standard, discovers items that don't conform, and rejects them as defects (see Figure 3-2).

**Key Point**

Of course, this is better than allowing defective products to go out to the customer. But the fact is, *judgment inspection does not reduce the number of defects*. There are two reasons for this:

1. Judgment inspection discovers defects only after they have been made. It does not prevent the defects from occurring.

2. Judgment inspection generally happens at the end of the process or after several operations are done. This means that there are built-in delays in the time it takes to discover a defect. In the meantime, the process creates more defective products. And sometimes this information never gets back to the place where the problem began.

---

## TAKE FIVE

Take a few minutes to think about these questions and to write down your answers:

- What are the four basic elements of ZQC? What role does each element play in avoiding defects?

- What is judgment inspection? Does this type of inspection occur in your workplace? When is it done?

---

# Informative Inspections Reduce Defects

Key Term

*Informative inspections* overcome the second problem of judgment inspections by giving feedback to the process that produces the defect. In an informative inspection, the focus is on alerting the defect-producing process (either the operator/assembler or the machine) about the problem as quickly as possible so that the problem can be corrected.

There are three ways to perform an informative inspection:

1. Statistical quality control (SQC)

2. Successive check of each product

3. Self-check of each product

Informative inspections help reduce defects, but they don't prevent them entirely. The next sections describe how the three types of informative inspection work.

Figure 3-3: SQC Gives Information about Process Errors, But Usually Too Late

## Statistical Quality Control (SQC)

Key Term

The *statistical quality control (SQC)* approach to inspection is to check samples of the product after processing to determine whether they are acceptable. When the sample shows a problem, information is fed back to the process so that the problem can be corrected. Usually a control chart is made to track the results of this checking over time.

SQC is better than a mere judgment inspection because it gives information back to the process. However, since SQC relies on samples rather than checking every unit, it does not ensure that 100 percent of the products are good. And, although information is recorded about the units that are checked, feedback and corrective action are often slow (see Figure 3-3).

## Successive Checks

Key Term

One way to improve on SQC inspections is to use successive checks. In a *successive check*, people in the next process inspect each unit that is passed to them. If they find a defect, they tell the previous person right away so that it can be corrected before too many more defects occur (see Figure 3-4, top).

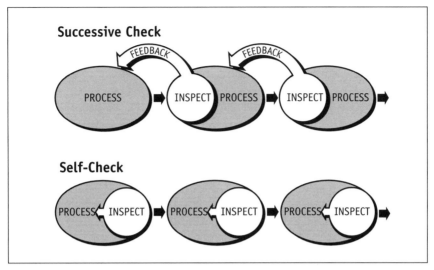

Figure 3-4: Successive Checks and Self-Checks Give Feedback about Defects

## Self-Checks

Key Term

Feedback and defect correction can happen even quicker when operators or assemblers themselves do a self-check. In a *self-check*, the operator or assembler checks his or her own work afterward for defects (see Figure 3-4, bottom). Self-checks give quicker feedback than successive checks; however, they can't catch all the defects. We're only human, after all, and sometimes it's hard to see our own mistakes as easily as someone else can. As a result, sometimes we miss things.

---

### TAKE FIVE

Take a few minutes to think about these questions and to write down your answers:

• How does an informative inspection differ from a judgment inspection?

• What are the three types of informative inspection? Do you use any of these in your process?

---

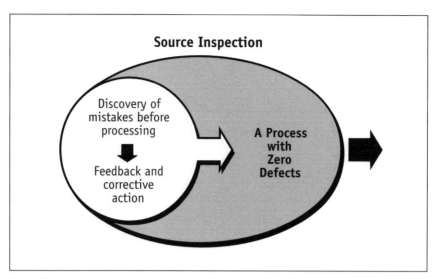

Figure 3-5: Source Inspection Keeps Errors from Turning into Defects

As you have learned, the self-check is the most effective type of informative inspection in terms of how quickly the information gets back to the place where the defect occurred. *Notice, however, that in all three types of informative inspection people are dealing with defects after they occur, not preventing them in the first place.* The only kind of inspection that can actually prevent defects is source inspection.

## Source Inspection Keeps Errors from Becoming Defects

Recall that source inspection is one of the four basic elements of the ZQC system. Source inspection differs from judgment inspection and informative inspection in a big way: *It catches errors — and gives feedback about them — before processing, so the errors don't turn into defects.* This is the integration of Check and Do stages we talked about: Something controls the doing so that it cannot be done wrong (see Figure 3-5).

Figure 3-6: When You Inspect Every Single Product, No Defects Can Slip By

Example

Source inspection might use a switch that halts the equipment if a part is fed in upside down, or a pin that physically prevents insertion of a workpiece the wrong way. Source inspection might also involve a warning light or sound that signals if operation is attempted before the equipment has reached proper operating conditions (such as temperature).

## 100 Percent Inspection Catches All Errors

Key Point

*The second unique element of the ZQC system is that it does a source inspection on every single product.* This is different from statistical quality control (SQC) inspections we discussed earlier, which usually rely on inspecting only a sampling of the product.

Although statistical sample-checking methods can give an idea whether the process is in control, they neither prevent defects nor guarantee that only a statistical number of defects will occur. Furthermore, SQC methods assume that a certain level of defects is unavoidable. This is inconsistent with the goal of zero defects, so ZQC uses methods that check 100 percent of the products (see Figure 3-6).

Figure 3-7: ZQC Inspections Mean Fast Feedback

## A Short Feedback Loop Means Quicker Action on Problems

Key Point

*The third element of ZQC is quick feedback so that errors can be corrected right away.* Traditional inspection methods don't do this very well. They happen after the process—when the errors have already turned into defects. In some situations (judgment inspection) they may not even tell the process it has made bad products. When they do inform the process (informative inspection), time has already passed—either the process has churned out more defects, or the conditions that caused the initial defect no longer exist and can't be learned from.

In ZQC the inspection is carried out by a system that signals the operator or assembly person about mistakes and machine errors before they become defects. This way, the situation can be fixed right away (see Figure 3-7).

## Poka-Yoke Systems Catch Errors We Might Have Missed

The fourth element that is unique to the ZQC approach is the use of mistake-proofing systems called *poka-yoke*. Rather than relying on operators to catch their own errors or those of the previous process, ZQC *uses poka-yoke devices installed in the machine to do source inspection and give quick feedback 100 percent of the time.*

**Key Point**

Poka-yoke systems use electronic sensors or passive devices to make sure inspection happens realiably. Most poka-yoke systems are inexpensive and can be built from simple parts. The best ideas for how to apply them often come from operators and assembly workers. Chapter 4 will describe the different types of poka-yoke devices and give some ideas for how to use them in your workplace.

---

### TAKE FIVE

Take a few minutes to think about these questions and to write down your answers:

- How does source inspection differ from traditional types of inspection?

- How might you use source inspection and the other three ZQC elements to prevent defects in your workplace?

---

# In Conclusion

### SUMMARY

ZQC prevents defects by combining four basic but unique approaches: source inspection, 100 percent inspection, immediate feedback, and the use of poka-yoke devices.

In judgment inspection, a person or machine simply compares the product with a standard, discovers items that don't conform, and rejects them as defects. In informative inspection, the focus is on informing the defect-producing process of a problem so that the problem can be corrected. There are three types of informative inspection: statistical quality control (SQC), successive checks, and self-checks.

Source inspection, the first element of the ZQC system, differs from judgment inspection and informative inspection in a big way: It catches errors of the equipment or the operator—and gives feedback about them—before processing, so the errors don't turn into defects.

The second element of a ZQC system is 100 percent inspection. In other words, a source inspection takes place on every single product, not just a statistical sampling. The third element of ZQC is quick feedback so that errors can be corrected right away, not after the process has churned out more defects or conditions that caused the initial defect no longer exist and can't be learned from.

Finally, the fourth element of a ZQC system is the use of mistake-proofing systems called poka-yoke. Rather than relying on operators or assemblers to catch their own errors or those of the previous process, ZQC uses poka-yoke devices installed in the machine to detect errors people might have missed.

## REFLECTIONS

Now that you have completed this chapter, take five minutes to think about these questions and to write down your answers:

- What did you learn from reading this chapter that stands out as particularly useful or interesting?

- Do you have any questions about the topics presented in this chapter? If so, what are they?

- What information do you still need to fully understand the ideas presented in this chapter?

# Chapter 4

# Using Poka-Yoke Systems

# About Poka-Yoke Systems

Recall from Chapter 3 that poka-yoke systems use sensors or other devices installed in processing equipment to detect errors that might slip by the operator or assembler. Poka-yoke systems are used to carry out two key elements of ZQC: 100 percent inspection and quick feedback for corrective action.

When a poka-yoke system detects an error, it automatically shuts down the equipment or gives a warning. How effectively it prevents defects depends on whether it is used for source inspection during the process or for an informative inspection after the process.

## Poka-Yoke Systems in Source Inspections

Key Point

*A true ZQC implementation means that poka-yoke systems are used in source inspections* to catch errors before the production process creates a defective product.

## Poka-Yoke Systems in Informative Inspections

Key Point

*Poka-yoke systems can also be used in informative inspections* where the check happens immediately after the process—either at the process as a self-check or at the next process as a successive check. An informative inspection will not eliminate all defects, but it can keep the defects from being passed down the line. This approach is more effective than statistical sampling or no feedback at all in reducing defects.

This chapter will describe the various types of poka-yoke systems, the main methods for using them, and the different types of sensing devices that can be used to detect abnormalities. Examples of poka-yoke systems will be presented in Chapter 5.

Figure 4-1: A Control System Stops the Equipment When an Error Happens

## How Poka-Yoke Systems Regulate the Process

Poka-yoke systems regulate the production process and prevent defects by using one of two approaches:

Key Term

1. A *control system* stops the equipment when an irregularity happens, or locks a clamp on the workpiece to keep it from moving on when it is not completely processed.

Key Term

2. A *warning system* signals the operator to stop the machine or address the problem.

Key Point

*A control system is more certain as a zero defects method because it doesn't depend on the operator* — the equipment stops itself when it detects a problem (see Figure 4-1). However, it is not always possible or convenient to set up a control system that stops the equipment automatically. In such cases, a warning or alarm system is used to get a person's attention — a flashing light or sound of some kind, for example. Control systems often use lights and sounds also, since the equipment needs attention to correct the problem.

Color-coding of parts, parts holders, and so on is a non-automated kind of warning system that can be very effective in catching errors.

**TAKE FIVE**

Take a few minutes to think about these questions and to write down your answers:

- How does a poka-yoke system work?

- Why are control systems more certain to prevent defects than warning systems?

# Methods for Using Poka-Yoke Systems

There are three main methods for using poka-yoke systems:

1. Contact methods

2. Fixed-value methods

3. Motion-step methods

Each of these methods can be used with either control systems or warning systems. Each method uses a different approach for dealing with abnormalities. It may be useful to think about these different methods as you consider what kind of system would prevent defects for your particular process.

## Contact Methods

Key Term

*Contact methods* work by detecting whether a product makes physical or energy contact with a sensing device.

Example

One example of a physical contact method would be limit switches that are pressed when screws are attached to a product (see Figure 4-2). The switches are connected to cylinders that hold the product in place until all the switches have been pressed. If a screw is left out, the product will not be released to the next operation.

Contact methods may also be energy sensing devices like photo-electric beams that don't physically touch the product but sense when something is not in the expected position.

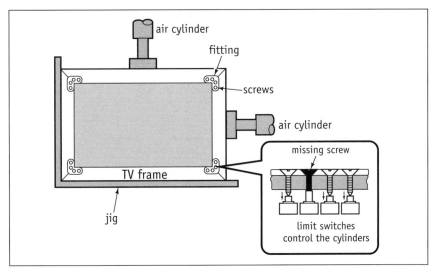

Figure 4-2: An Example of a Contact Method for Using Poka-Yoke Systems

**Key Point**

Contact methods do not have to be high tech. *Some of the best contact methods are "passive devices"* such as guide pins or blocks that don't allow the product to be seated in a machine jig in the wrong position.

**Key Point**

*Contact methods often take advantage of parts that are designed with an uneven shape,* such as a workpiece with a bump or a hole on only one end. Using a passive jig that matches the shape, or a limit switch positioned to detect an abnormal shape, this approach signals right away if the workpiece is not positioned correctly for processing. Small design changes can often make it a lot easier to catch errors. Problems you notice during processing can help designers improve product and equipment design for mistake-proofing in the future.

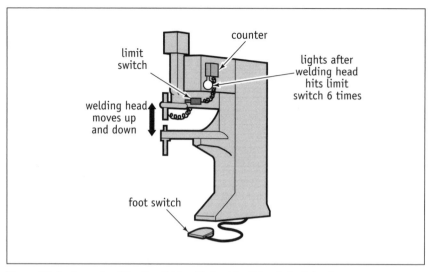

Figure 4-3: An Example of the Fixed-Value Method for Using Poka-Yoke Systems

## Fixed-Value Methods

Key Term

*Fixed-value methods* can be used when a fixed number of parts must be attached to the product or when a fixed number of repeated operations needs to be done at a process station. In this method, a device counts the number of times something is done and signals or releases the product only when the required number is reached.

**Example**

The fixed-value method may use switches such as limit switches that are tripped with each movement, sending a signal to a counter that detects when the right number of movements has happened (see Figure 4-3). Another approach is to measure or count the number of parts in advance; if parts are left over, the operator will know that some have been left out.

## Motion-Step Methods

Key Term

The third approach to setting up poka-yoke systems is the *motion-step method*. This method is used to sense whether a motion or step in the process has been carried out within a certain expected time, such as a machine's cycle time. It can also be used to ensure that things happen according to a certain sequence, which avoids errors.

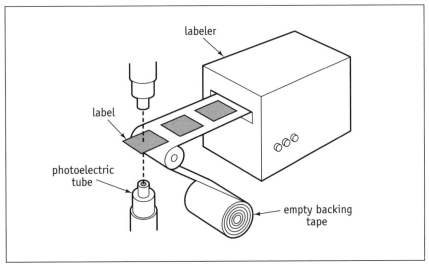

Figure 4-4: An Example of the Motion-Step Method for Using Poka-Yoke Systems

Example

The motion-step method uses sensors and devices like a photo-electric switch connected to a timer. If a movement doesn't happen when it should, the switch signals to stop the equipment or give a warning. For example, a label-dispensing machine uses a photoelectric switch to stop the line if it does not detect removal of a label within the machine's cycle time (see Figure 4-4).

Example

The "sequencing" aspect of the motion-step method is frequently used to help assemblers select the right parts for the particular product model they are putting together. The illustration on the cover of this book shows this approach: When the system reads a code on a card, the right parts bins are indicated.

---

## TAKE FIVE

Take a few minutes to think about these questions and to write down your answers:

- In what kinds of situations in your workplace might you use contact-method poka-yoke devices? Fixed-value method? Motion-step method?

- Can you think of ways to use "passive" contact methods such as pins, blocks, etc.?

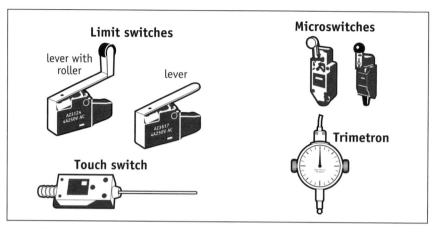

Figure 4-5: Examples of Physical Contact Sensing Devices

# Types of Sensing Devices

The sensing devices used in poka-yoke systems can be divided into three broad categories:

- Physical contact sensing devices

- Energy sensing devices

- Sensors that detect changes in physical conditions

Each type of sensor includes a wide range of devices that can be used in different situations. Let's take a closer look at some of these sensing devices.

### Physical Contact Sensing Devices

Key Term

*Physical contact sensing devices* work by physically touching the product or machine part. In many cases, particularly in automated processes, physical contact sensing devices send an electrical signal when they are touched. The signal can stop or start a machine or give a warning.

Examples of physical contact sensing devices are shown in Figure 4-5. Let's briefly discuss a few of them.

Key Term

*Limit switches* and *microswitches* are among the most common (and least expensive) types of physical contact sensing devices. They are used to confirm the presence and position of objects that touch the small lever on the switch.

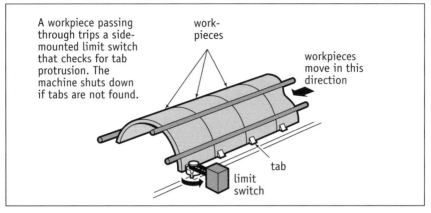

A workpiece passing through trips a side-mounted limit switch that checks for tab protrusion. The machine shuts down if tabs are not found.

work-pieces

workpieces move in this direction

tab

limit switch

Figure 4-6: An Example Using a Limit Switch as a Poka-Yoke Device

Example

Limit switches and microswitches can be used to detect product parts feeding into a machine in the wrong position or without being processed (see Figure 4-6). They can also detect broken tools or parts that could cause defects. Since they are small, microswitches can be used in tight spaces in the equipment.

Key Term

A *touch switch* is similar to a limit switch in function, but it is activated by a light touch on a thin "antenna." Touch switches can detect with high sensitivity whether an object such as a product or machine part is present, properly positioned, broken, or of the proper dimensions.

Key Term

A *trimetron* is a sensitive, needle-type gauge that sends signals to sound an alarm or stop equipment when the conditions it measures are not within acceptable limits. Trimetrons can also open and close sorting gates to automatically separate acceptable products from unacceptable ones.

## TAKE FIVE

Take a few minutes to think about these questions and to write down your answers:

- What are three types of sensing devices used in poka-yoke systems?

- Can you think of situations in your workplace in which physical contact sensing devices would be useful? How?

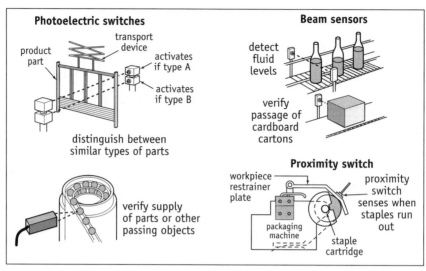

Figure 4-7: Some Uses of Photoelectric Switches, Beam Sensors, and Proximity Switches

## Energy Sensing Devices

Key Term

*Energy sensing devices* use energy rather than physical contact to determine whether an error is occurring.

A *photoelectric switch* uses beams of light to inspect transparent objects, judge welds, and verify a variety of conditions such as:

- proper size or color of an item

- passage of objects on a conveyor

- proper supply of parts

- proper feeding of parts

*Beam sensors* use electron beams to detect, for example, the proper level of liquid in a container or the passage of an object on a conveyor.

Example

A *proximity switch* responds to changes in distance from objects and to changes in magnetic force. For this reason, it can be used with magnetically sensitive materials. For example, a proximity switch might shut down a machine and sound an alarm when it detects that a supply of magnetically sensitive parts has run out.

Applications of photoelectric switches, beam sensors, and a proximity switch are illustrated in Figure 4-7 above.

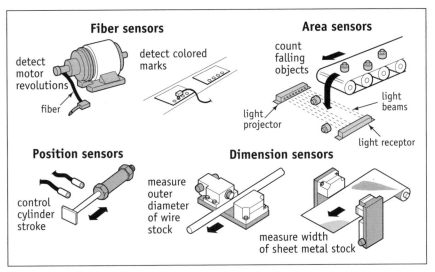

Figure 4-8: Examples of Energy Sensing Devices

Other types of energy sensing devices and typical uses include:

- *Fiber sensors*: detect motor revolutions, color coding marks, or marks on translucent objects or printed matter.

- *Area sensors*: detect random breaks in a fixed area, such as hands placed in hazard areas or parts dropping from a conveyor.

- *Position sensors*: control cylinder strokes or determine screw heights.

- *Dimension sensors*: ensure correct product dimensions.

- *Vibration sensors*: detect product ejection errors, width distortion, seam position, or start of processing.

- *Displacement sensors*: detect and measure warping, thickness, and fluid level heights.

- *Tap sensors*: detect incomplete tap screw machining.

- *Metal passage sensors*: detect metal in motion.

- *Color-mark sensors*: detect colored marks or differences in color.

- *Double-feed sensors*: detect two products fed at the same time.

- *Weld position sensors*: detect joints such as weld lines in coil stock, seams in pipes and cans, or splices in wires.

Some applications of these devices are illustrated in Figure 4-8 on this page and on page 48. The chart on page 49 (Figure 4-9) gives a summary of physical contact and energy sensing devices and what they detect.

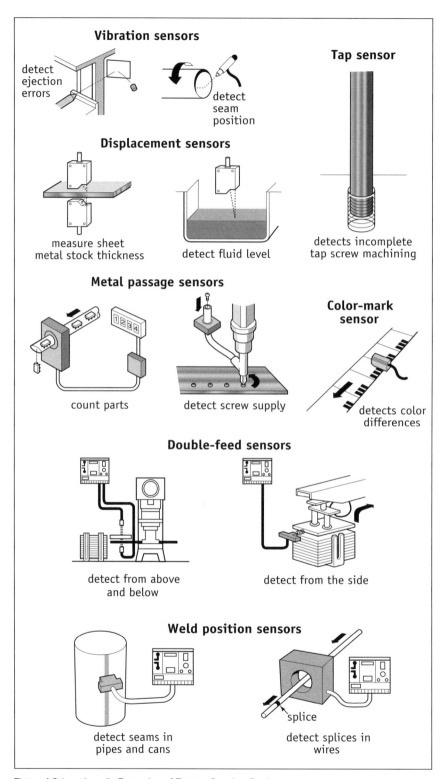

**Vibration sensors**

detect ejection errors

detect seam position

**Tap sensor**

detects incomplete tap screw machining

**Displacement sensors**

measure sheet metal stock thickness

detect fluid level

**Metal passage sensors**

count parts

detect screw supply

**Color-mark sensor**

detects color differences

**Double-feed sensors**

detect from above and below

detect from the side

**Weld position sensors**

detect seams in pipes and cans

splice

detect splices in wires

Figure 4-8 (continued): Examples of Energy Sensing Devices

| Types of Sensors | Presence | | | Confirmation of Position | Measurement | Overlap | Shape | Foreign Matter | Damage | Color Mismatch |
| | Passage | | Break | | | | | | | |
| | line | plane | | | | | | | | |
|---|---|---|---|---|---|---|---|---|---|---|
| **Physical Contact Sensing Devices** | | | | | | | | | | |
| limit switches | ● | | ● | ● | ● | | | | | |
| microswitches | ● | | ● | ● | ● | | | | | |
| touch switches | ● | | ● | ● | ● | ● | | | | |
| trimetrons | | | | | ● | | | | | |
| **Energy Sensing Devices** | | | | | | | | | | |
| photoelectric switches — transmission types | ● | | ● | ● | ● | | | | | |
| photoelectric switches — reflection types | ● | | ● | ● | ● | ● | | | ● | ● |
| beam sensors — transmission types | ● | | ● | ● | ● | | | | | |
| beam sensors — reflection types | ● | | ● | ● | ● | ● | | | ● | ● |
| proximity switches | ● | | ● | ● | ● | ● | | | | |
| fiber sensors | ● | | ● | ● | ● | ● | ● | | | ● |
| area sensors | ● | ● | | | | | | | | |
| position sensors | | | | ● | | | | | | |
| dimension sensors | | | | ● | ● | | ● | | | |
| vibration sensors | ● | | ● | ● | | | | | | |
| displacement sensors | ● | | | ● | ● | ● | | | ● | ● |
| tap sensors | | | | | ● | | | | | |
| metal passage sensors | ● | ● | | | | | | ● | | |
| color-mark sensors | ● | | | ● | | | | | | ● |
| double-feed sensors | ● | | | | | ● | | | | |
| weld position sensors | | | | ● | ● | | ● | | | |

Figure 4-9: Types of Sensors and Their Functions

## Sensors That Detect Changes in Physical Conditions

Key Term

A third type of poka-yoke sensors, known as *condition change sensing devices*, detects changes in physical conditions. This group can be divided into three broad categories:

- pressure
- temperature
- electrical current

Pressure changes can be detected by pressure gauges and pressure-sensitive switches. These devices can be used to detect problems like oil supply interruptions.

Temperature changes can be detected through the use of heat-activated devices such as thermometers, thermostats, thermistors, and the like. These can be used to check surface temperatures of dies, electronic parts, and motors. They can also be used to perform machine maintenance checks and other kinds of industrial temperature measurement control.

Changes in electrical current flow include meter relays, which can control the causes of defects by detecting the occurrence of electrical currents. Another device, called a current eye or nugget tester, monitors weld strength by detecting secondary voltage changes in the weld points.

# Devices That Link to Poka-Yoke Sensors

**Key Point**

*In addition to the sensing devices themselves, poka-yoke systems often include devices that link to the sensors.* These devices detect abnormalities in the system that might cause an error, or transmit information about errors.

For example, *counters* are used to keep track of the number of motions or operations, as signaled by limit switches or other sensing devices. They can be set to signal a control or warning device if the normal number does not occur.

*Timers* are used when a motion or operation is expected to happen within a certain time. Like counters, they are usually linked to a sensing device and also to a control or warning device. Sometimes timers and counters are used together, as well.

**Key Point**

*Information-transmitting devices* include warning devices that use sound or lights to draw attention to abnormalities. *Keep in mind that a sound usually calls attention to the problem more quickly than a light does.* When a light is used, remember that the "summoning power" of a flashing light is far greater than that of a steady light. Some warning systems use both light and sound.

---

### TAKE FIVE

Take a few minutes to think about these questions and to write down your answers:

- Can you think of situations in your workplace in which energy-sensing devices and sensors that detect changes in physical conditions might be useful? How?

- What about devices that link to poka-yoke sensors? Which of these might be helpful in your work and why?

---

# In Conclusion

## SUMMARY

Poka-yoke are systems installed in machines to detect errors that might slip by the operator or assembler. Poka-yoke systems are used to carry out two key elements in ZQC: 100 percent inspection and quick feedback for corrective action.

A true ZQC implementation means that poka-yoke systems are used in source inspections to catch errors before the production process creates a defective product. Poka-yoke systems can also be used in informative inspections where the check happens immediately after the process. This will not eliminate all defects, but it can keep the defects from being passed down the line.

Poka-yoke systems regulate the production process by using one of two approaches: (1) a control system, which stops the equipment, or (2) a warning system, which signals someone to address the problem. A control system is more certain as a zero defects method.

There are three main methods for using poka-yoke systems: contact methods, fixed-value methods, and motion-step methods. Each of these methods can be used with either control systems or warning systems.

Contact methods work by detecting whether a product makes physical or energy contact with a sensing device. Contact methods often take advantage of uneven shapes in the product's design. They include passive methods such as guide pins, as well as sensors such as limit switches.

Fixed-value methods count the number of times something is done and signals or releases the product only when the required number is reached. Motion-step methods sense whether a predetermined motion or step in the process has been carried out within a certain expected time, such as a machine's cycle time, or in a certain sequence.

## SUMMARY – cont'd

The sensing devices used in poka-yoke systems can be divided into three broad categories: physical contact sensing devices, energy sensing devices, and devices that sense changes in physical conditions.

Physical contact sensing devices work by physically touching the product or machine part. In many cases, they send an electrical signal when they are touched. The signal either stops the machine or gives a warning. Examples of physical contact sensing devices include limit switches, micro-switches, touch switches, and trimetrons.

Energy sensing devices use energy rather than physical contact to determine whether an error is occurring. Examples include photoelectric switches, beam sensors, proximity switches, fiber sensors, area sensors, and displacement sensors.

As the name implies, condition change sensing devices detect changes in physical conditions such as pressure, temperature, and electrical current flow. Examples include pressure gauges and pressure-sensitive switches, thermometers and thermistors, meter relays, and nugget testers.

In addition to the sensing devices themselves, poka-yoke systems often include devices that link to the sensors. These devices detect abnormalities in the system that might cause an error, such as counting or timing abnormalities. Other devices, such as buzzers, lights, and flashing lights, transmit information about errors. Sound usually calls attention to the problem more quickly than a light does. When a light is used, the "summoning power" of a flashing light is far greater than that of a steady light.

## REFLECTIONS

Now that you have completed this chapter, take five minutes to think about these questions and to write down your answers:

- What did you learn from reading this chapter that stands out as particularly useful or interesting?

- Do you have any questions about the topics presented in this chapter? If so, what are they?

- What information do you still need to fully understand the ideas presented in this chapter?

- How can you get this information?

# Chapter 5

# Examples of Poka-Yoke Applications

# Learning from Examples of Poka-Yoke Applications

In this chapter we present numerous examples of poka-yoke systems used in real-world applications. *The purpose of this chapter is to expose you to a variety of applications, which will in turn help you understand how poka-yoke systems are used.* These examples may also give you some ideas about how to apply poka-yoke systems in your own workplace.

Look at the next page and notice that it is divided into a "Before Improvement" section and an "After Improvement" section. Each example in this chapter will be presented in the same format. To get the most out of the examples, we suggest that you cover up the "After Improvement" section on each page until you have read the "Before Improvement" section. This way, you can think about the problem and how you might approach it, based on what you learned about poka-yoke systems in Chapter 4, before you read about how the problem was actually solved.

Once you have thought about the problem on your own, then read the "After Improvement" section and study the pictures. Can you think of other ways to handle the same problem?

Finally, *notice as you study the examples that a poka-yoke system need not be fancy and expensive.* In fact, many of the solutions are actually quite simple and inexpensive. Many of these solutions were suggested by equipment operators and assemblers—the people who know the machines and processes the best. As you read the chapter, think about how a poka-yoke system might help your own process become error-free.

# Poka-Yoke Systems Used in Source Inspection

## Catching an Incorrectly Positioned Workpiece

### Before Improvement

This operation attaches a brake wire to a clamp. The assembly person places the clamp into a U-shaped jig, which holds it while the wire is inserted. The problem is that there are two kinds of clamps—one for the left side and one for the right side. These parts are not interchangeable. However, both kinds of

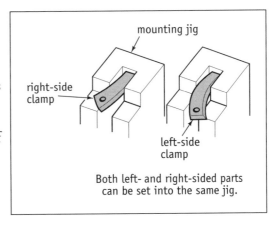

mounting jig

right-side clamp

left-side clamp

Both left- and right-sided parts can be set into the same jig.

clamps fit into the same jig, so it is easy to mistakenly mount a left-side clamp when the instructions call for a right-side clamp.

**What would you do to prevent this mistake?**

### After Improvement

The operation now uses two different jigs that are specific for right-side clamps and left-side clamps. These jigs were made from the old jigs simply by installing a block on each one that doesn't allow the wrong kind of clamp to seat properly in that jig. This passive poka-yoke device prevents accidental processing of the wrong clamp.

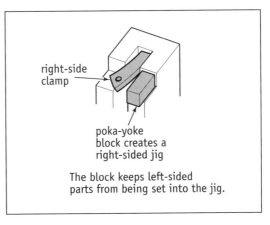

right-side clamp

poka-yoke block creates a right-sided jig

The block keeps left-sided parts from being set into the jig.

## Contact Method: Catching an Incorrectly Positioned Workpiece

### Before Improvement

The square workpieces have a set of holes punched in them by a turret punch press. Next, each workpiece is set in a jig on a drill press, where more holes are drilled.

Even though one end of the workpiece has more punched holes than the other, it is easy to accidentally turn the piece around the wrong way as it is placed in the drilling jig because the workpiece is a square. When this error is not caught in time, it results in defective products that are drilled in the wrong place.

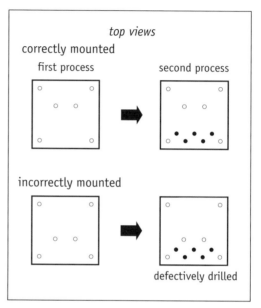

*top views*

correctly mounted

first process → second process

incorrectly mounted → defectively drilled

### What would you do to prevent this mistake?

### After Improvement

A pin that corresponds to one of the punched holes is installed on the drilling jig. Since these holes are supposed to be on one end of the workpiece and not on the other, the pin keeps the workpiece from seating in the jig unless the holes are on the correct end. This stops the problem of drilling the products in the wrong position.

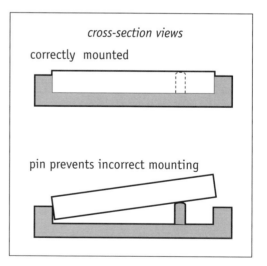

*cross-section views*

correctly mounted

pin prevents incorrect mounting

## Contact Method: Detecting Unprocessed Parts in a Chute

### *Before Improvement*

Molded parts are milled in an automatic machine, then fed to the next process by way of a chute. Sometimes a processing error allows an unmilled part to leave the milling machine and come down the chute. When an unmilled part enters the machine for the next process, it stops the machine and sometimes damages it.

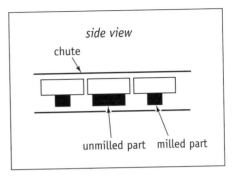

### What would you do to prevent this mistake?

### *After Improvement*

A method was devised to use the shape of the unmilled parts to stop them in the chute before they reached the machine. This involves placing two small blocks in the chute in such a way that the thin "stem" of the milled parts can pass through, but the thicker "stem" of an unmilled part catches on the blocks and doesn't go any further. The operator then removes the unmilled part and restores the flow of milled parts into the machine.

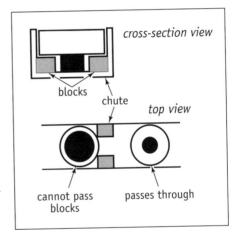

## Contact Method: Ensuring Proper Positioning of Blanks for Stamping

### Before Improvement

This example involves an automatic line for stamping house number plates. The blank plates used for this process sometimes catch on the edge stops that are supposed to position them for stamping. When the stamping is carried out with a blank in this improper position, defects are created.

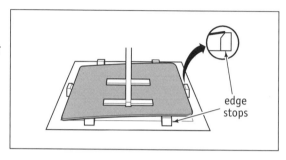

### What would you do to prevent this mistake?

### After Improvement

Proximity switches are mounted on the edge stops on the two sides where the blanks sometimes catch. When a blank is properly positioned, it trips both proximity switches, allowing the machine to start. If a blank catches on an edge stop, it does not trip the switch, and the machine will not start.

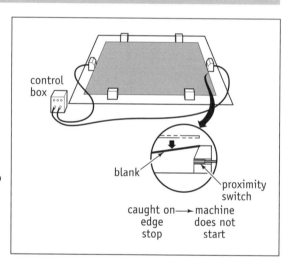

## Contact Method: Detecting Wrong Position of Bonded Metal Parts

### Before Improvement

Parts made of bonded steel and aluminum are fed into a machine for forming. In this process, the steel side is supposed to face upward. However, sometimes a part goes into the forming machine with the

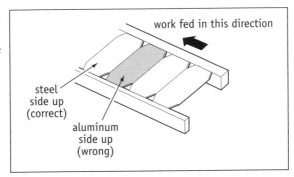

work fed in this direction

steel side up (correct)

aluminum side up (wrong)

aluminum side up, which damages the tools in later processes and holds up production.

### What would you do to prevent this mistake?

### After Improvement

A proximity switch is installed above the parts that are fed into the machine. The switch is set to detect the steel when it is a certain distance from the sensor. When a part has the aluminum side up, the steel is farther away, so the switch does not operate. This causes the equipment to shut down and sound a warning.

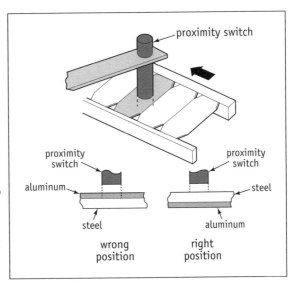

proximity switch

proximity switch

aluminum

steel

wrong position

proximity switch

steel

aluminum

right position

## Contact Method: Catching Mispositioned Parts in a Press

### Before Improvement

A part is placed in a press for forming. The part has a protruding neck on one side that is supposed to be in a certain position, but sometimes the part is processed with the neck in the wrong position. This creates a defect.

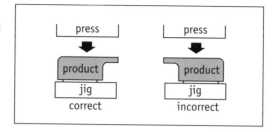

### What would you do to prevent this mistake?

### After Improvement

A limit switch is installed on the press jig onto which the part is placed for processing. The switch is positioned so that it turns the machine on only when the neck on the part is positioned where it is supposed to be.

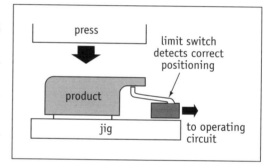

## TAKE FIVE

Take a few minutes to think about these questions and to write down your answers:

• Can you think of situations in your workplace where contact poka-yoke devices could be useful in a source inspection?

• How would you describe the causes of the problems in these examples? Can you think of other ways to solve them?

## Fixed-Value Method: Preventing Omitted Welds

### Before Improvement

A portable spot welder is used to make ten different welds on an automotive part. Sometimes some of the welds are missed accidentally.

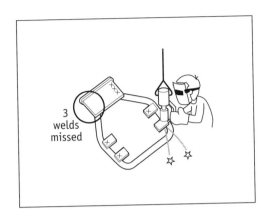

### What would you do to prevent this mistake?

### After Improvement

The part that is being welded is clamped in place by an air cylinder, which is controlled by a control board equipped with a counter. The counter does not allow the clamp to release the part until it counts that the welder has been operated ten times, indicating that all ten welds have been made.

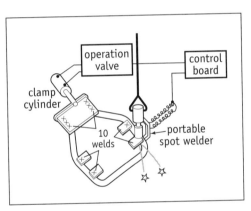

## Fixed-Value Method: Reminding People to Change Welding Tips

### *Before Improvement*

The tip on a welding machine wears out with use. It needs to be changed after a certain number of welds so that the diameter of the welded area stays within specifications. Sometimes, however, people forget to change the tips when they are supposed to. This results in defective products.

counter

4000

number of welds

I'm likely to forget

---

**What would you do to prevent this mistake?**

---

### *After Improvement*

A control board uses a counter to keep track of how many welds the machine makes. When the critical number of welds has been made (in this example, 4,000), the control board stops the machine and flashes a light to signal an employee to change the tip.

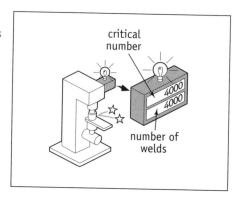

critical number

4000
4000

number of welds

64

## Fixed-Value Method: Making Sure All Bolts Are Installed

### *Before Improvement*

In assembly of an automobile spoiler, nine mounting bolts are to be installed. The bolts are taken directly out of a bin containing many bolts, and sometimes some of the bolts are forgotten.

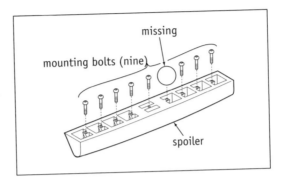

### What would you do to prevent this mistake?

### *After Improvement*

This assembly operation now uses a parts feeder that automatically counts out nine bolts when a lever is pressed. The assembler hold the bolts in one hand while installing them with the other. The spoiler does not leave this station until all nine bolts have been installed.

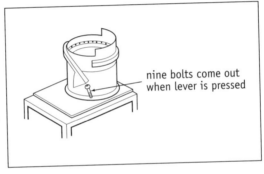

## Fixed-Value Method: Avoiding Omission of Insulation Tape

### Before Improvement

Insulation tape is applied to television cabinets in ten locations. The tape is supplied in strips lined up on a rod and is taken off as

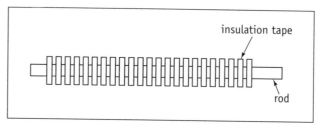

needed and applied to the cabinet. Sometimes the assembly people forget to apply some of the strips, resulting in a defective cabinet.

### What would you do to prevent this mistake?

### After Improvement

The tape strips are now supplied in groups of ten. If one of the locations is missed, it will be clear because a tape strip will remain on the rod.

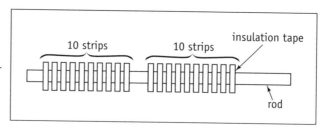

## TAKE FIVE

Take a few minutes to think about these questions and to write down your answers:

• Can you think of situations in your workplace where fixed-value poka-yoke devices could be useful in a source inspection?

• How would you describe the causes of the problems in these examples? Can you think of other ways to solve them?

## Motion-Step Method: Avoiding Assembly with Wrong Parts

### *Before Improvement*

An auto parts assembly operation involves installing several parts, which vary from model to model. The parts are taken from bins according to a list of parts for each model. Sometimes the wrong part is installed by mistake, or parts are forgotten.

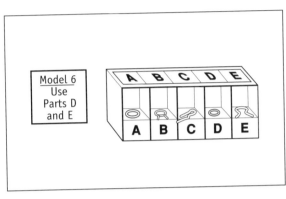

### *What would you do to prevent this mistake?*

### *After Improvement*

Doors and lights are installed on the parts bins and wired to a model indicator board. When the assembly person pushes the number for the current model on the indicator board, the doors open for the bins holding the proper parts, and lights above the bins make sure that the assembler sees all of the parts needed for that model.

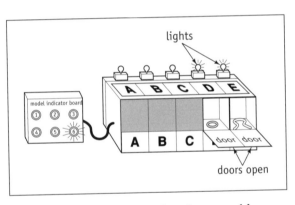

## Motion-Step Method: Preventing Omitted or Doubled Washers

### Before Improvement

In an automotive assembly operation, a washer is attached to another part. The washers are supplied in a box and taken out by the assembler. Although this is done carefully, sometimes washers are omitted or doubled.

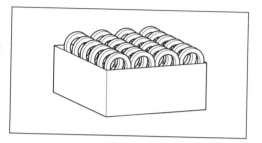

### What would you do to prevent this mistake?

### After Improvement

A device is made that feeds a single washer when the assembly machine is turned on. The washer stops on a small platform and is picked up and installed by the assembler. If the washer is forgotten, it will be pushed onto a catch tray by the next washer that is pushed out, alerting the assembler. Washers cannot be doubled because the device will not feed another washer until the assembly machine is turned on.

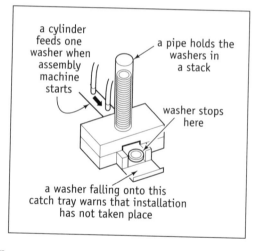

a cylinder feeds one washer when assembly machine starts

a pipe holds the washers in a stack

washer stops here

a washer falling onto this catch tray warns that installation has not taken place

## TAKE FIVE

Take a few minutes to think about these questions and to write down your answers:

• Can you think of situations in your workplace where motion-step poka-yoke devices could be useful in a source inspection?

• How would you describe the causes of the problems in these examples? Can you think of other ways to solve them?

# Poka-Yoke Systems Used in Informative Inspections

## Contact Method: Catching Uncut Bolts Before Further Processing

### Before Improvement

An automated machine is used to cut grooves under the heads of certain bolts. Sometimes a machine error results in bolts that do not have the grooves cut. A visual inspection is done after the process, but

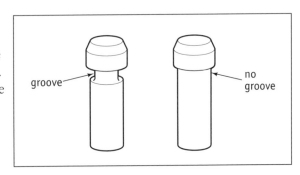

this is not completely effective, and ungrooved bolts are occasionally sent to the next process.

**What would you do to prevent this mistake?**

### After Improvement

The chute through which the bolts leave the machine is modified with a pair of plates that act as a passive poka-yoke device. If a bolt is properly processed, the grooved part will slip through the two plates and on to the next process. If the groove has not been cut, the bolt will hit the plates and stop. This triggers an alarm

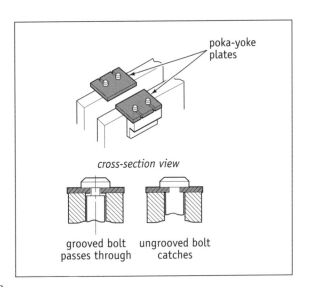

so that the operator can pull out the unprocessed piece, correct the machine's condition, and cut the required groove.

## Contact Method: Ensuring Adequate Testing of Solder Joints

### Before Improvement

The strength of a solder joint on a lighting fixture part is tested afterward by pulling on the lead wires. This test is not reliable, however; different people have different pulling strength, and sometimes they forget to do the test. Both situations allow weakly soldered parts to pass on to the next process.

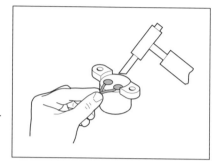

### What would you do to prevent this mistake?

### After Improvement

A jig now holds the part stationary while the soldering is done. This jig holds the part in place using springs that press steel balls firmly against the part. Testing is accomplished simply by pulling on the lead wires to remove the part from the jig. If the wires come out of the solder when pulled against the resistance of the springs, they are resoldered to the part.

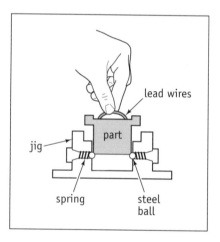

## Contact Method: Testing for Uncut Grooves

### Before Improvement

The process involves cutting oil grooves in a particular product. Due to tool changes and damaged bits, products without grooves are missed sometimes in inspection and are sent to the customer, who returns them with a complaint.

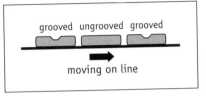

grooved ungrooved grooved

moving on line

**What would you do to prevent this mistake?**

### After Improvement

A device is installed at the next process to test for the presence of the oil grooves. The device uses

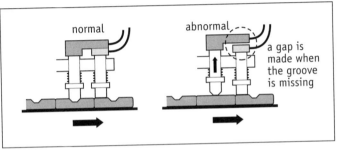

normal

abnormal
a gap is made when the groove is missing

two spring-loaded pins that are linked above by a simple interlocking circuit mechanism. One pin is set for the height of the ungrooved area of the product, and the other pin is set for the height of the grooved area. When the groove is present, both pins move together and the equipment keeps moving. When no groove is present, the groove-detecting pin is pushed up, making a gap in the interlocking circuit and shutting down the machine.

## TAKE FIVE

Take a few minutes to think about these questions and to write down your answers:

- Can you think of situations in your workplace where contact poka-yoke devices could be useful in an informative inspection?

- How would you describe the causes of the problems in these examples? Can you think of other ways to solve them?

## Fixed-Value Method: Inspecting for Missing Staples on Cases

### Before Inspection

A packaging machine puts together corrugated cases in which products are shipped. The cases are fastened with heavy-duty staples on the top and bottom flaps. Sometimes the machine runs out of staples or jams and does not insert the staples. It is easy to inspect the top flaps for staples, but it is very difficult to verify that the staples are present on the bottom flaps—where they are needed most.

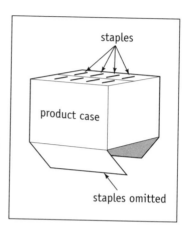

### What would you do to prevent this mistake?

### After Improvement

Metal-detecting sensors and counters are mounted where the case exits the packaging machine. When these devices do not detect the right number of staples, a stopper comes up and keeps the case from moving on.

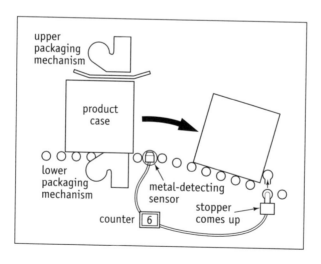

## Motion-Step Method: Making Sure a Second Operation Is Performed

### Before Improvement

A particular assembly operation on a washing machine involves tightening two kinds of screws, using two different air-powered drivers that hang from the ceiling. Sometimes people forget to use the second air driver, which means products move to the next process without being properly tightened.

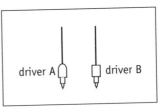

**What would you do to prevent this mistake?**

### After Improvement

The cords for the two air drivers are now linked by a horizontal rod with a heavy metal ring threaded on it. When driver A is pulled down and used, the ring slides to one end

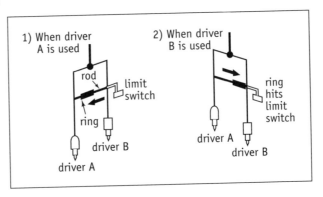

of the rod. When the assembler pulls down driver B, the ring slides to the other end and hits a limit switch to signal that the operation is complete. This system uses a timer; if the limit switch is not hit within the usual cycle, a warning sound is made.

### TAKE FIVE

Take a few minutes to think about these questions and to write down your answers:

- Can you think of situations in your workplace where fixed-value or motion-step poka-yoke devices could be useful in an informative inspection?

- How would you describe the causes of the problems in these examples? Can you think of other ways to solve them?

# In Conclusion

## SUMMARY

Examples of poka-yoke systems as they are used in real-world applications are presented in this chapter. Examples help you understand how poka-yoke systems are put to use. They may also give you ideas about how to apply poka-yoke systems in your own workplace.

Poka-yoke systems need not be fancy or expensive. Many of the solutions presented in this chapter are actually quite simple and inexpensive. Also, many of the solutions were suggested by equipment operators and assemblers—the people who know the machines and processes the best. How can poka-yoke systems help your own process become error-free?

## REFLECTIONS

Now that you have completed this chapter, take five minutes to think about these questions and to write down your answers:

- What did you learn from reading this chapter that stands out as particularly useful or interesting?

- Do you have any questions about the topics presented in this chapter? If so, what are they?

- What information do you still need to fully understand the ideas presented in this chapter?

- How can you get this information?

# Chapter 6

## Reflections and Conclusions

### CHAPTER OVERVIEW

**Reflecting on What You've Learned**

**Applying What You've Learned**

- Possibilities for Applying What You've Learned
- Your Personal Action Plan

**Opportunities for Further Learning**

**Conclusions**

**Other Resources Related to ZQC
and Mistake-Proofing**

# Reflecting on What You've Learned

An important part of learning is reflecting on what you've learned. Without this step, learning can't take place effectively. That's why we've asked you at the end of each chapter to reflect about what you've learned. And now that you've reached the end of the book, we'd like to ask you to reflect on what you've learned from the book as a whole.

Take ten minutes to write down answers to the following questions:

- What did you learn from reading this book that stands out as particularly useful or interesting?

- Do you have any questions about ZQC or mistake-proofing? If so, what are they?

- What ideas, tools, and techniques have you learned that will be most useful in your own work? How will they be useful?

- What ideas, tools, and techniques have you learned that will be least useful in your work? Why wouldn't they be useful?

# Applying What You've Learned

## Possibilities for Applying What You've Learned

The way you decide to apply what you've learned will, of course, depend on your individual situation. If your company is launching a full-scale ZQC implementation program, you should have ample opportunity to apply what you've learned right away. In this case, you may be included on a team of people who are responsible for implementing ZQC in a certain work area. Or you may have implementation time structured into your work day and may be responsible for reporting the results of your activities on a regular basis.

On the other end of the spectrum, your company may have no immediate plans to implement ZQC. In this case, the extent to which you can implement what you've learned will depend on how much control you have over your own schedule, work flow, and work area.

## Your Personal Action Plan

Whatever your situation, we suggest you create a personal action plan for how you will begin applying the information you have learned from this book. You might start by referring to your own notes about the techniques and tools you think will be most useful to you, then writing down answers to the following questions:

- What mistake-proofing techniques can I implement right now that will make my job easier, better, or more efficient?

- How can I involve my coworkers in the implementation of what I've learned?

When you've answered these questions, we suggest that you commit to completing the things you've written down in a specific period of time, and to making a new plan at the end of that time period.

It's often good to start with something small that you can comfortably finish in the time you've allowed yourself. If the project is too ambitious or time-consuming you can easily get discouraged and give up.

# Opportunities for Further Learning

Here are some ways to learn more about ZQC and mistake-proofing:

- Find other books or videos on this subject. Several are listed on the next page.

- If your company is already implementing ZQC, visit other departments to see how they are using mistake-proofing techniques and tools.

- Find out how other companies have implemented ZQC.

# Conclusions

ZQC is more than a series of techniques. It is a fundamental approach to error-free production. We hope this book has given you a taste of how and why this method can be helpful and effective for you in your work. Productivity Press welcomes your stories about how you apply ZQC in your own workplace.

# Other Resources Related to ZQC and Mistake-Proofing

The following resources will provide you with additional education about various aspects of mistake-proofing and poka-yoke systems. All resources except the last are available from Productivity Press.

S. Shingo, *Zero Quality Control: Source Inspection and the Poka-Yoke System* (Productivity Press, 1986)—This is the sourcebook for *Mistake-Proofing for Operators*. It includes the story of how ZQC was developed, basic principles and reasoning behind the elements of ZQC, a detailed introduction to poka-yoke devices, and many examples of application of these devices in different situations.

The Productivity Press Development Team, *Mistake-Proofing for Operators Learning Package* (Productivity Press, 1996)—This package is designed to help you lead an employee learning group in your company using *Mistake-Proofing for Operators* as the reading material. Each package includes the sourcebook *Zero Quality Control: Source Inspection and the Poka-Yoke System*, a *Leader's Guide*, overheads, slides, and five copies of *Mistake-Proofing for Operators*.

*The Poka-Yoke System*—A video program that shows how Shingo's ZQC approach works to eliminate defects at their source. The program covers the theory and conceptual stages of ZQC and poka-yoke systems, as well as practical shopfloor applications. Includes two-part printed guide.

NKS/Factory Magazine, ed., *Poka-Yoke: Improving Product Quality by Preventing Defects* (Productivity Press, 1988)—A 28-page overview, which describes the nature of errors and how poka-yoke devices prevent them, is followed by 240 illustrated examples of poka-yoke devices in action. Indexes to improvement categories, operations, parts and products, and detection methods help readers find helpful ideas for their own operations.

Omron Electronics, Inc., *Sensor Guidebook* (Omron Electronics, 1995)—A catalog and guidebook for photoelectric and proximity sensors, timers, and counters that includes helpful descriptions of how the methods work, guidance on which methods to use for various situations, and suggested solutions for specific detection needs. (Request from Omron's Marketing Communications Division, Schaumburg, IL, fax 1-847-843-7787.)

# About the Authors

## Shigeo Shingo

Shigeo Shingo was born January 8, 1909 in Saga City, Japan. His career spanned over 50 years in factory improvement methodology. He is considered a cofounder (with Taiichi Ohno) of Toyota Motor Company's just-in-time production system.

From 1976 until his death in 1990, Dr. Shingo consulted and lectured widely, inspiring senior managers and factory workers alike throughout Europe and the United States. He wrote nearly 20 books, many of which have been published in English by Productivity Press. In 1988 he was awarded honorary Doctor of Management degrees by Utah State University and by the Université de Toulouse in France. In that year he designated Utah State University to award the annual "Shingo Prizes for Manufacturing Excellence" to North American businesses, students, and researchers.

## The Productivity Press Development Team

Since 1981, Productivity Press has been finding and publishing the world's best methods for achieving manufacturing excellence. At the core of this effort is a team of dedicated editors and writers who work tirelessly to deliver to our customers the most valuable information available on continuous improvement. Their various backgrounds—art history, English literature, graphic design, instructional design, law, library science, psychology, philosophy, and publishing—provide a breadth of knowledge and interests that informs all their work. They love beautiful books and work together to create designs that please as well as ease our readers' use of our books. They read endlessly to keep up on new terminology and changes in both the manufacturing and the publishing industry. They learn from our customers' experiences in order to shape our books and off-the-shelf products into effective tools that serve our customers' learning needs.

# Continue Your Learning with In-House Training and Consulting from Productivity, Inc. Client Services Group

## Consulting Services

For over a decade, an expansive client base continues to recommend Productivity's Consulting Services to colleagues eager to accelerate their improvement efforts. We have established a lasting improvement process with companies from various industries, including textiles, printing and packaging, chemicals, and heavy equipment.

Assignments vary from results-driven trainings on the tools of Lean Production, to broad total company conversion projects dealing with strategic intent through organization design/redesign. Tailoring our methodology to accommodate site-specific organizational and performance considerations is a real strength of Productivity's Consulting Services.

## Educational Resources

Our products and services are leading-edge, and have been used by most every company in the Fortune 500 and beyond. Topics include: Quick Changeover, Visual Workplace, Lean Production Systems, Total Productive Maintenance, and Mistake-Proofing.

We offer the following opportunities to enhance your improvement efforts: National Conferences, Training Events, Plant Tours, Industrial Study Missions, Master Series Workshops, and Newsletters.

Call the Productivity, Inc. Client Services Group and learn how we can provide Consulting Services and Educational Resources customized to fit your changing needs.

**Telephone: 1-800-966-5423 (U.S. only) or 1-203-846-3777
Fax: 1-203-846-6883**

# LEARNING PACKAGE

The Learning Package is designed to give your team leaders everything they need to facilitate study groups on *Mistake-Proofing for Operators*. Shopfloor workers participate through a series of discussion and application sessions to practice using the tools and techniques they've learned from the book.

*The Learning Package:*

- Provides the foundation for launching a full-scale implementation process
- Provides immediate practical skills for participants
- Offers a flexible course design you can adapt to your unique requirements
- Encourages workers to become actively involved in their own learning process

*Included In Your Learning Package:*

- Five copies of *Mistake-Proofing for Operators*
- One copy of *Zero Quality Control: Source Inspection and the Poka-Yoke System*
- One 8-1/2" x 11" Leader's Guide
- A set of overhead transparencies that summarize major points
- A set of slides with case study examples

**Mistake-Proofing Learning Package**
The Productivity Press Development Team
ISBN 1-56327-128-1
Item # ZQCLP-B271

# About the Shopfloor Series

*Put powerful and proven improvement tools in the hands of your entire workforce!*

Progressive shopfloor improvement techniques are imperative for manufacturers who want to stay competitive and to achieve world class excellence. And it's the comprehensive education of all shopfloor workers that ensures full participation and success when implementing new programs. The Shopfloor Series books make practical information accessible to everyone by presenting major concepts and tools in simple, clear language and at a reading level that has been adjusted for operators by skilled instructional designers. One main idea is presented every two to four pages so that the book can be picked up and put down easily. Each chapter begins with an overview and ends with a summary section. Helpful illustrations are used throughout.

*Other books currently in the Shopfloor Series include:*

**QUICK CHANGEOVER FOR OPERATORS**
**The SMED System**
The Productivity Press Development Team
ISBN 1-56327-125-7 / incl. application questions / 93 pages
Item # QCOOP-B271 / $25.00

**5S FOR OPERATORS**
**5 Pillars of the Visual Workplace**
The Productivity Press Development Team
ISBN 1-56327-123-0 / incl. application questions / 133 pages
Item # 5SOP-B271 / $25.00

**TPM FOR EVERY OPERATOR**
Japan Institute of Plant Maintenance
ISBN 1-56327-080-3 / 136 pages
Item # TPMEO-B271 / $25.00

**TPM FOR SUPERVISORS**
The Productivity Press Development Team
ISBN 1-56327-161-3 / 96 pages
Item # TPMSUP-B271 / $25.00

**TPM TEAM GUIDE**
Kunio Shirose
ISBN 1-56327-079-X / 175 pages
Item # TGUIDE-B271 / $25.00

**TO ORDER:** Phone toll-free **1-800-394-6868** (outside the U.S., **503-235-0600**), fax toll-free **1-800-394-6286** (outside the U.S. 503-235-0909), e-mail **service@ppress.com**, or mail to Productivity Press, Dept. BK, P.O. Box 13390, Portland, OR 97213-0390. Send check or charge to your credit card (American Express, Visa, MasterCard accepted). For U.S. orders add $5 shipping for first book, $2 each additional for UPS surface delivery; international customers must call for a quote. We offer attractive quantity discounts for bulk purchases of individual titles; call for more information.

See the Productivity Press online catalog at http://www.ppress.com

# READING

## THE FOUNDATIONAL SKILL OF THE KNOWLEDGE WORKER

In keeping with our vision as "The Education Company for the Knowledge Era", Productivity Press is proud to announce our affiliation with READ RIGHT, a company specializing in workforce literacy. If members of the workforce in your company have difficulty reading this book, we recommend you consult READ RIGHT for assistance.

 ### Read Right—Specializing in Workforce Literacy
*Eliminating employee reading problems yields hidden benefits*

A breakthrough that helps employees quickly eliminate reading problems and improve English communication skills is yielding very encouraging side benefits. Not only are graduates of READ RIGHT able to read and understand training materials, safety signs, equipment manuals, and other written communications—they also realize new feelings of self-confidence and self-esteem. This translates into greater willingness to become involved in team meetings. With new skills and self-confidence, workers participate, speak up, and contribute ideas as never before.

*"We see people who were once reluctant to participate on teams for Total Quality Improvement projects now stepping up. I see people coming out of their shells and coming forward with more improvement ideas. I can think of no other training we have done or are doing that will make a greater contribution to improving the performance of our mills than READ RIGHT."*

— Otto Lueschel, Vice President, Manufacturing, Weyerhaeuser, Western Lumber Division

New knowledge about how the brain learns the reading process has enabled READ RIGHT to develop a fundamentally new way to teach reading that cuts the time necessary to eliminate employees' reading problems by over 90%. READ RIGHT is also effective in teaching English communication skills to employees for whom English is a second language.

**For more information on how READ RIGHT might benefit your employees and your company, please phone 1-800-427-9440.**